The Odyssey of a Film-Maker

THE ODYSSEY

published by Beta Phi Mu · 1960

OF A FILM-MAKER

Robert Flaherty's Story

by Frances Hubbard Flaherty

PREFACE

According to Webster's definition a chapbook "is any small book containing ballads, tracts, etc., such as were formerly carried about for sale by chapmen; hence any small book of popular literature."

In defiance of old meanings and standards, Beta Phi Mu presents THE ODYSSEY OF A FILM-MAKER *as the fourth in its series of chapbooks—none of which has been truly small or popular, or hawked in the streets by chapmen, and none of which has contained tracts or ballads.*

When this international library science honorary society was founded a decade ago, its membership decided that in addition to recognizing scholarly achievements within the profession, the organization would also play an active role in furthering the art of book design. It was felt that this could best be done by issuing a series of publications in which the designer would be given complete freedom to experiment. Thus was launched the Beta Phi Mu Chapbook Series, the subject matter of which has ranged from book design to fine bindings, from the juvenilia of H. G. Wells to this personal record of Robert Flaherty.

The text which follows grew out of a number of talks which Frances Flaherty gave, during which film clips from the great Flaherty films were used to accompany her remarks. No one else, of course, knew Robert Flaherty as well as Frances Hubbard, who became his wife in 1914 and shared with him the triumphs and frustrations of his creative years. She

5

accompanied her husband on expeditions to Samoa, the Aran Islands, India, and Louisiana. Although she often had three children in tow, she took on the duties of still photographer during three of these movie-making journeys. Some of her experiences are recorded in her books, Samoa and Elephant Dance.

Designer of Chapbook Number Four is Bert Clarke, who has been in design and printing since 1935. He has designed books for a number of publishers, is a former production manager for the Limited Editions Club, and is co-director of the Thistle Press.

Beta Phi Mu would like to express its appreciation to Henry L. Mueller for bringing the fraternity and Frances Flaherty together, as well as for suggestions and advice concerning the scope of the manuscript.

"Poetry, on the other hand, being exploratory . . ."

Herbert Read:
"Poetic Consciousness and
Creative Experience."
Eranos Jahrbuch, 1956

I

I SHALL SPEAK to you of Robert Flaherty's method, because this method and the way it came to be is, I believe, the important legacy he left us, and because for me it was the great experience of my life with him. And also because his films themselves do not give evidence of a method, that is of an apparatus of film-making and its devices. I remember Sir Carol Reed saying to me, "When I look at other people's films I can usually tell exactly how they have arrived at their effects; in your husband's films I cannot tell at all." And a student writing her thesis on "The Films of Robert Flaherty and Their Critics" remarked that many critics had said much the same thing: that they found a "sort of magic" in the films and could not tell what that magic was.

Magic, the thing we cannot understand, we tend to write off as "genius." But what we write off, history in its own good time writes in again, no longer as magic, but as the science which it has become.

To begin with a brief summary:

Robert Flaherty made three biographies of peoples—*Nanook of the North* of the Eskimos, *Moana* of the Polynesians, and *Man of Aran* of islanders living off the coast of Ireland. They have been called Films of the Spirit of Man. All have the same theme—the spirit with which these people come to terms with their environment. History from age to age has been written in the spirit of peoples, as it is being written now in our spirit. And what Robert Flaherty is saying in these three films he has told us himself in a talk he gave for the British Broadcasting Corporation. "Nanook's problem was how to live with nature. Our problem is how to live with our machines. Nanook found the solution of the problem in his own spirit, as the Polynesians did in theirs. But we have made for ourselves an environment that is difficult for the spirit to come to terms with. Our problem still goes on." In *The Land*, a film he made for the Agriculture Department of the United States Government, he asks the question: "When will man learn to live with his machines? These miraculous machines! A new world stands before us, a world beyond our dreams. The great fact is the land, the Land itself and the People, and the Spirit of the People." The power of our great machines to transform the world Robert Flaherty saw as an extension of our own spirit. *The importance of the new machine, the motion-picture camera, was its power to change that spirit, to transform us in ourselves.*

"When you talk about your husband's work," a good friend advised me, "don't try to say too much, but hammer home the one thing you are really talking about, the one thing that really matters. Put it all into one word and keep to that, keep saying it. Make it clear that your talk is not a memorial to Robert Flaherty, but a call—his call, if you like—to one particular thing."

The word I have chosen is "non-preconception," an explorer's word. Non-preconception is the pre-condition to discovery, because it is a state of mind. When you do not preconceive, then you go about finding out. There is nothing else you can do. You begin to explore.

"All art," said Robert Flaherty, "is a kind of exploring. To

discover and reveal is the way every artist sets about his business."
The explorers, the discoverers, are the transformers of the world.
They are the scientist discovering new fact, the philosopher discovering in new fact new idea. Above all, they are the artist, the
poet, the seer, who out of the crucible of new fact and new idea
bring new life, new power, new motive, and a deep refreshment.
They discover for us the new image.

"Discovery," writes L. L. Whyte in his book, *The Next Development in Man*, "is the essence of social development, and a
method of discovery its only possible guarantee."[1] Non-preconception, a method of discovery as a process of film-making, was
Robert Flaherty's contribution to the motion picture. From that
method everything there is in his films flows.

Robert Flaherty is known as "The Father of Documentary,"
and it is true that he was the first to fashion his films from real life
and real people. But a Flaherty film must not be confused with
the documentary movement that has spread all over the world,
for the reason that the documentary movement (fathered not by
Robert Flaherty but by a Scotsman, John Grierson) was from its
beginning all preconceived for social and educational purposes,
just as many of our most famous films have been preconceived for
political purposes, for propaganda, and, as Hollywood preconceives,
for the box office. These films are timely, and they serve, often
powerfully and with distinction, the timely purposes for which
they were made. But there are other films, and the Flaherty films
are among these, that are timeless. They are timeless in the sense
that they do not argue, they celebrate. And what they celebrate,
freely and spontaneously, simply and purely, is the thing itself for
its own sake. They are timeless in the sense of the Mohammedan
prayer which says, "O, God, if I worship Thee in fear of Hell, burn
me in Hell; or if I worship Thee in hope of Paradise, exclude me

1. Whyte, L. L.: *The Next Development in Man*. New York, Holt, 1948, p. 138.

from Paradise; but if I worship Thee for Thine Own Sake, withhold not Thine Everlasting Beauty."

It was as an explorer that Robert Flaherty came into films, and not until he was forty years old. As he said, "I was an explorer first and a motion picture maker a long way after." His explorations took him into the North, into Hudson Bay. On four expeditions over a period of six years he made two crossings of the largest unknown land mass left in that part of the world, rediscovered islands in the Bay that had been lost since the time of Henry Hudson, and became, as his friend and fellow-explorer, Peter Freuchen, said of him, "*The* great name in Canadian subarctic exploration."

These years of exploration in the North with the Eskimos were Robert Flaherty's motion-picture school. From the Eskimos he learned to see as he had not seen before.

Robert Flaherty had himself the keen eyes of an explorer, trained to read the signs in a landscape, but the Eskimo has eyes keener still, for on that great white screen which is his world the Eskimo must be instantly aware of every movement, every least shadow of movement that might mean game, food, life. And if visibility is blotted out, as it so often is, his other senses must take over, for his commitment to life is total, and his orientation must be total. The passing moment becomes the fullness of life and its fulfillment—becomes, as on the motion-picture screen, the moment of truth.

The teaching of the North was its immensity, its vast simplicity, its emptiness, unclutteredness, its clarity and purity, and its elemental strength, wind and snow endlessly carving new worlds of hazard and beauty—of a mysterious, mystical beauty. I once asked Bob why he wanted to go back and back again to that country and its hardships. For a long moment he was thoughtful. I was waiting for him to counter with something about its beauty. He

The kayak—Nanook's hunting boat.

Nanook: How the white man "cans" his voice.

Nyla, "The Smiling One"—Nanook's wife.

The omiak—the women's boat.

To be a great hunter like his father.

said simply, "I go to come back." In that life up there, there was something he found that was for him a deep refreshment, a profound renewal.

On his third expedition into the Bay his chief, Sir William Mackenzie, said to him, "Why don't you take up with you one of those newfangled things called a motion-picture camera?" Why not indeed? He could make a film of these remarkable people, the Eskimos. If he showed them on the screen just as they were, perhaps others would feel about them as he felt, see as he saw their fine spirit.

Eagerly he shot off 70,000 feet of film, took it to Toronto to edit, and then, "Amateur that I was," he said, "I dropped a lighted cigarette on it and it went up in flame. But I wasn't sorry. It was a bad film; it was dull—it was little more than a travelogue. I had learned to explore, I had not learned to reveal." His subject he knew and loved; no one could have known and loved it better. What he did not know yet was his instrument, his camera. He was determined to go back.

With a partial print of the burned film under his arm, for two years Robert Flaherty trudged the streets of New York. Finally persuading Revillon Frères, the French furriers, to finance him, he went again into the Bay, met Nanook, mighty hunter of the Itivimuit tribe of Eskimos, and there on the bleak, barren coast of the Bay, half-way to the North Pole, in a one-room hut snow-walled to the eaves in winter, he began his thirty years' research of the motion-picture camera. For, this time, he took up with him, besides his camera and film, a developing, printing, and projecting outfit, so that he could see what he was getting as he went along, what his camera was doing, what it *could* do, what the capacities were of this new machine.

He had the Eskimos to help him—Nanook and three others: Wetaltook, Tookalook, and Little Tommy. They did everything for him. They brought water for developing the film, chiseling six feet down through river ice and bringing it in barrels sloshing with ice and deer hair that fell into it from their fur clothing. They strained it and heated it. They built a drying reel out of driftwood, combing the coastline for miles to pick up enough wood to finish it. When Bob's little electric light plant failed to give a light steady enough for printing, they blacked out a window all but a bit the size of a single motion-picture frame, and through this slot Bob printed his film, frame by frame, by the light of the low arctic sun. The cameras fell into the sea and had to be taken apart, cleaned, and put together again. Fortunately, the Eskimo has, naturally, an exceptional mechanical gift. When Bob couldn't put his Graflex together (it has a complicated shutter) he turned all the scattered parts of it over to Tommy, and Little Tommy put them together for him.

But the Eskimos had no idea whatever what all this they were doing was about. They had never seen a film. Give them a still picture to look at, and, like as not, they would hold it upside-down. So one day Bob threaded his projector, pinned a Hudson's Bay blanket on the wall, and invited them all in, men, women, and children. He had taken a picture of Nanook spearing a walrus, the walrus fighting in the surf to get away, and Nanook on shore struggling to drag him in while the cow walrus came and locked tusks with her mate in a desperate effort to pull him free.

The projector light shone out. There was complete silence in the hut. They saw Nanook. But Nanook was there in the hut with them, and they couldn't understand. Then they saw the walrus, and then, said Bob, pandemonium broke loose. "Hold him!" they screamed. "Hold him!" and they scrambled over the chairs and each other to get to the screen and help Nanook hold that walrus!

From then on there was no talk of anything but more hunting scenes for the "aggie," as they called the picture. There was one scene particularly which became an obsession with Nanook, and that was a bear hunt. He knew where the bears were denning, giving birth to their young. It was easy, he said, to find a den by its vent with the steam coming out. With his snow knife he would cut the vent open, the enraged mother would rush out rearing, the dogs would engage her, she would toss them hurtling through the air, and then, said Nanook, "With my spear I will close in. Wouldn't that make a fine 'aggie'?" Bob said it would, and they started off for the bear country.

It was an ill-fated journey. Bad weather set in, and there was no game, no seal, no food for the dogs and the men. The dogs grew weak; one dog died. They stopped, built an igloo, and while Bob huddled in his sleeping bag and the dogs huddled in the igloo tunnel, the men went off to hunt. Day after day passed, and still there was no game. Even the sea-birds were dying, lying frozen on the ice. The men themselves were losing strength. Every morning Bob would offer them what was left of the last of his own food, but Nanook wouldn't touch it. At last one night the men came back, and by the crunch of their feet on the snow Bob knew that they were bringing something. Behind them they were dragging a seal, and it was a big square-flipper. The dogs were fed; the men gorged and then slept. Through the night, said Bob, from their warm bodies curlicues of steam spiralled up into the cold air. In the morning they were able to travel again.

It was cold work, filming, so cold that sometimes the film, when threaded into the camera, shattered like so much glass. Nanook would have to carry it inside his fur clothing next to his warm body, the same place where he warmed Bob's feet when they were cold. The coldest time of all, Bob remembered, was after the long day's sledging, waiting in the bitter wind and drifting snow for Nanook to build the igloo. One night, caught by a blizzard, that hour of waiting was almost more than he could bear. At last, the

15

final block of the igloo in place, on the heels of Nanook he crawled in. Nanook lit a candle. Around and above them the snow dome "sparkled and glittered and glistened like the dust of diamonds." Nanook's face broke into a smile. He turned to Bob. "Surely," he said, "no house of the *Kablunak* (the white man) could be so wonderful."

After a year in the North and almost as many months in New York editing his film, Bob brought it to the distributors. A distributor must now be found to buy it or the public would never see it, never know that there was such a film. He took it to them all, one after the other, and one after another they all turned it down. Not by the farthest stretch of the imagination, said they, could such a film ever be box-office. They didn't even trouble to return the print, and Bob had humbly to rummage for it and salvage it from a scrap heap.

Often Nanook had laughed at Bob—how foolish he was to take so much trouble to make a film of them who were certainly the commonest people in the world! But Bob had a prescience about his film. Up there in the Bay, sitting with Nanook on the cobbled shore waiting for the Hudson's Bay steamer that was to take him out—Nanook very sad because now there would be no more hunting for the film and there were so many more wonderful hunting scenes they still could make—Bob comforted him, saying, "You see these pebbles? As many *kablunat* (white men) as there are pebbles on this beach will see Nanook and his family."

Nanook was finally taken for distribution by a French newsreel company, Pathé Frères. Two French firms, Pathé Frères and Revillon Frères, got together and made a deal. Pathé wanted to cut the film up into newsreels. Revillon prevailed upon them to take it whole.

Two years later Nanook was dead—as so many of his people die—of starvation. Storm-bound while hunting in the interior, he had not been able to reach the coast and its life-giving seal in time. But by that time *Nanook*, the film, had gone around the world, and Nanook, the Eskimo hunter, had become a world character, world-beloved. News of his death came out in the press as far away as China and Japan. In Malaya there was a new word for "strong man," and it was "Nanuk." Ten years later in Berlin, in the Tiergarten, I bought an Eskimo pie. It was called a "Nanuk," and Nanook's face smiled up at me from the wrapper.

Such was the impact of this first film of its kind, made without actors, without studio, story, or stars, just of everyday people doing everyday things, *being themselves.*

That was in 1922, and now in 1959 the film is still being shown. Where I live in Vermont I do not have television, but my neighbors do. Twice last year they called me up. "You'd better come over," they said. "They're showing *Nanook.*" What is the secret of the life of this very simple film? What is there about it that makes it endure? For commercially it is probably the most long-lived film that has ever been made.

I met two young German film directors a year or so ago, and when they told me that *Nanook* was still playing in Germany, I asked them, "Why do you think this is? How do you explain it?" One of them spoke up quickly, "It is because we can identify with these people on the screen."

Now, Hollywood wants us to identify with its stars: that is what the stars are for. But I do not think that is what those Germans meant—not identifying with Eskimos in that sense. I think they meant that our identification is with life itself, with universal life of which we and these people are a part. When Nanook and Nyla and little Allegoo smile out at us from the screen, so simple, so genuine and true, we, too, become simple, genuine, true. They are themselves: we, in turn, become ourselves. Everything that might separate us from these people falls away. In spite of all our differences, indeed the more because of them, we are one with these people. And that feeling of oneness can deepen and become a feeling of oneness with all peoples and all things. It can become that profound and profoundly liberating experience we call "participation mystique." But—and this is the point—let one false gesture, one least unnatural movement, the slightest hint of artificiality, appear, and separateness comes back. Again we are just looking *at* the people on the screen, and the whole experience of identity, of oneness, of participation, becomes impossible, could not happen, could never be. The secret of *Nanook* lies, I believe, in those two words, "being themselves." Not Acting, but Being.

II

THE SUCCESS of *Nanook* drew the attention of Hollywood. Paramount, the Famous Players-Lasky Corporation, indeed Jesse Lasky himself, came to Bob and said, "Go anywhere you want in the world. Write your own ticket. All you have to do is bring us back another *Nanook*."

Just then a friend of ours, Frederick O'Brien, published his book, *White Shadows in the South Seas*. It was a best seller. He had been living in a Samoan village. The village was beautiful; the people were beautiful; there you could see as much as you could see anywhere of the old Polynesian life. "Go," he said to Bob, "to the village of Safune on the island of Savai'i and you may still be in time to catch that beautiful old culture before it passes entirely away."

So we went to Samoa, the whole family this time: Bob, his brother, David, our three small daughters, an Irish nursemaid, and myself.

This time we were making a film for Hollywood, and we were very conscious of that fact. Bob had no illusions whatever as to what Paramount expected of him in the way of thrills and sensations for the box office. All the way down on the steamer we talked about it, conjured up this scene and that scene, imagining the sea monsters we might find lurking in the deep-sea caverns under the coral reefs that fringe the islands. When one day a report came in from another ship at sea that one of these monsters had been sighted —a giant octopus, its tentacles spread over the waters from a body the size of a whale—we were sure that we were on the right track.

Bob lost no time. No sooner had we landed than he began to search for giant octopi and tiger sharks. For weeks and weeks he searched and searched, combed the islands from end to end. When finally he had to admit that they simply were not there, I remember the miserable weeks and weeks he just sat on our veranda with every thought falling away from him, learning the first hard lesson of what it takes to make a *true* film of a subject you do not know: that you cannot preconceive. If you preconceive you are lost, off to a false start before you begin. What you have to do is to let go, let go every thought of your own, wipe your mind clean, fresh, innocent, newborn, sensitive as unexposed film to take up the impressions around you, and let what will come in. This is the pregnant void, the fertile state of no-mind. This is non-preconception, the beginning of discovery.

Meanwhile our own personal life had been becoming highly dramatic, because of the people's excitement about us. Before our arrival on the island, our equipment, about sixteen tons of boxes and bales, had been dumped on the shore, all marked up for insurance purposes with fantastic and, to the Samoans, fabulous values. They drew their own conclusions: Bob was an "American millionaire," he was a very high chief in his own country. Promptly he was made a very high chief in Samoa. Now in Samoa the whole drama of life is played around the rank and prestige of its chiefs, and is celebrated endlessly in ritual and ceremony, with singing and dancing, feasting, and speech-making. Every high chief on the island must now drink kava, the ceremonial drink, with the great high chief from America. All over the island every village had to

Climbing for coconuts.

The Tufuga—the tattooing chief.

Making tapa cloth from the bark of the mulberry tree.

Moana dancing with his bride, Fa 'agase.

Tattooing of Moana.

bring out its singers to sing for us and its dancers to dance. Plantations were stripped to make great feasts for us, and the talking chiefs prepared hours-long speeches of welcome. These, we suddenly realized, were those age-old rites, the fabulous old Polynesian ways, that lovely pattern of human relations, we had come so far to film.

Bob gave himself over to the camera. We filmed and filmed. We went mad with filming, let the camera see everything and see it exhaustively. Two hundred and forty thousand feet of film reeled through the camera and out into a darkroom in an underground cave where two Samoan boys developed and printed it, and then would bring it, leaping and shouting through the village, calling out for all the village to hear how well they had "cooked" it, and, with a final ceremonial flourish, lay it as a food-offering at our feet.

Then we would project it, on a screen set up under the coconut palms, with all the village looking on, making the film with us, telling us what they thought, particularly the older chiefs who still remembered the old forgotten ways and could help us to recapture them and tell us if our film was true.

And so it was that day by day and week by week and month by month the picture on the screen began to grow, began taking on a life of its own.

I remember sitting on the deck of the steamer that was taking us home again, watching the last of our island sink below the horizon, thinking of our cans of film in the ship's hold. There was the old Polynesian culture we were leaving behind that was dying; but here it was, *living*, in those cans that we were taking away.

This miraculous machine! Life expressed in motion, ritual gestures, beautiful movements "worn smooth by time"—movements too fine for the eye to see, but that the camera could catch, and, catching them, could capture the very spirit of these people.

Just before we started for Samoa, we were given a dinner at the old Waldorf-Astoria. *Nanook* had been hailed not only as a new kind of film, but also as a new use of the motion picture. Films like this, with their truth and intimacy, their deeply personal appeal, would bring the peoples of the world together in better understanding, and would serve the cause of international relations in every country. The dinner was given for us by *Asia*, a magazine founded with the purpose of bringing East and West together. Distinguished representatives from government, big business, the arts and sciences, and the great foundations all made long and eloquent speeches on how films like these now should and would be made around the world. They gave us their blessing.

Two years later, we brought *Moana* back.

One of the old Polynesian customs that has died out almost entirely in Samoa is tattooing. In that idyllic country where Nature is kind, where food is ever ripening in the ground and on the trees, and life is easy, there is no conflict, no suffering, no pain. But where there is no suffering there is no strength. This, the people in their wisdom know, so they invent suffering—a painful ordeal. Tattooing is the courage, the pride, the dignity of the race which gives it grace to live.

Tattooing naturally became the climax of our film, and the critics hailed the new Flaherty film as "Frazer's *Golden Bough* brought to life," as "an epic of race . . . poetic, philosophic—lovely beyond compare . . ." But Paramount was appalled. They didn't know what to do with a film like this, entirely lacking in any of the box-office elements which *Nanook* had had. They decided to shelve the film, write it off as a total loss.

But Bob persuaded them first to try an experiment, to put the film out in six towns across the country for a trial run, and see what would happen. Then into each of these six towns, with the help of the National Board of Review he sent special advertising to a special list of literate townspeople. The result was that these people came to see the film in such numbers that in some cases they broke the theatre's box-office records. We had found our audience; the film was box-office after all! We were jubilant. But not for long; for we soon realized that the cost of such advertising all over the country for just one film was more than any motion picture company could be expected to bear.

So then, remembering the eloquent speeches at the Waldorf dinner, Bob bethought himself of the great foundations. Here was something for them, ready-made. A meeting was arranged, but what exactly transpired at that meeting I do not know. All I can say is that to it came a representative of the Hays organization, representing Hollywood. Films, the foundations were given to understand, were a business—Hollywood's business. Paramount finally put the film out to its regular customers in its regular way, as "the love life of a South Sea siren." Those who wanted to see the love life of a South Sea siren did not see what they wanted to see, and those who were waiting to see the new Flaherty film didn't know that this was it—and the film died at the box office. In Paris it ran for six months in one theatre. In Sweden there was a command performance for the Swedish Parliament, and a request for a copy for Sweden's archives. But in this country, where alone its commercial success could be assured, the integrity of the film had been its undoing.

III

FROM THEN ON Bob's filming became catch-as-catch-can. It was eight years before he had another film of his own to do. The hope of one more film like *Moana* did flare up, not from the great foundations, not from the arts and sciences, or government or big business—but from Hollywood again, another Hollywood company willing to take a chance, this time in our own Southwest, with our Southwest Indians, the vanishing cultures in our own land. And you who know that country and its breathtaking landscape, and the Indians, those people whose whole life, and the wholeness of it, is the living poetry and religion of that landscape, will understand how we felt when, after a year, the film was called off.

We took a ship for Europe. We might find opportunity there. On the way over, Bob fell into conversation with an Irishman. They talked about the Depression in America. "You should see," said the Irishman, "how the people in my country, the Aran Islanders, live. They even have to make their soil."

When, a year later in England, Michael (now Sir Michael) Balcon, of Gainsborough Studios, wanted to make a low-budget film somewhere in the British Isles, Bob told him the remarkable story he had heard about the Aran Islanders. Sir Michael found this story remarkable too, and we went to have a look at the Aran Islands. Well I remember the day we first saw those gray, barren, three-hundred-foot cliffs rising up out of the sea,—a day in November. The air was fresh, the water sparkling; dolphins were playing in it and beyond them the Twelve Bens of Connemara rose snow-capped into the clear blue of the sky. Clinging from generation to generation to these sea-swept rocks, the Aran Islander has met the challenge of the sea and come to terms with it. There is always a special feeling about a place where people have taken root. I remember how, as I dabbled abstractedly in the shining water lapping at my feet, there came over me a deep contentment, a sense of well-being that was like an enchantment. We could make a film here, somehow we knew.

We settled on Aranmore, the largest and farthest seaward of the three islands, midway on its lee shore beside a cove as round and shining as a silver dollar. We overlooked the white-capped bay and the fleets of little turf boats bobbing over from the mainland, their slanting sails looking like gulls, and hardly bigger than gulls, as they brought turf to this island without fuel. They would unload on the pier in our cove beside the fish-shed we had converted into a laboratory.

It was a never-ending delight to sit on the wharf-edge over the water and peer down into clear depths watching perhaps for a conger eel to show. One day two monsters came into the cove, two basking sharks. We saw them first as twin sail-like fins cutting the surface. Beneath the surface, their huge bodies thirty feet long, with white jaws open as they fed on plankton, we could reach down and touch with our hands as the curragh passed over them. This was an Aran wonder of which we had never been told. But now we heard the whole story of the Aranman's fight for the oil for his lamps in years not so long ago, harpooning these monsters from the prows of their pookawns as whales are harpooned, and often being towed far out to sea, sometimes not to be heard of again. The tales of the hunting of the basking shark, the largest fish in the world, had become legendary, for the great migrations had for some years ceased. Now here they were again! Old harpoons were still to be found in the rafters of Aran cottages, and there was an old man in Galway who as a boy had been taken out harpooning himself. Bob made a trip to Galway to see this old man, this source of vital information. He left no stone unturned. For the hunting of the basking shark had become for him, as had the hunting of the bear for *Nanook*, an obsession. He sent for books about the creature; he wrote to museums; he studied the medicinal properties of fish-liver oils. He had an old friend of his Hudson Bay days who had been a whaler. From his home in Dundee we called him, chartered a boat for him, rigged it for whaling, and when the next year one of the greatest shark migrations ever seen (announced by the look-outs we had set to watch for it) came into Galway harbor, we were ready for it.

But in the meantime, and first of all, we had to find our cast, gather together our Aran family. At first the people were shy of us and suspicious. They still remembered Cromwellian days when the Protestants coming from England had tried to make "soupers" of them, offering them soup to save them from starvation if they would change their religion. We were Protestants. Our name was Flaherty, to be sure, but how did they know we hadn't assumed it on purpose? It was rumored that in his pocket Bob carried a phial of a liquid which, if thrown upon any of them, would turn him into a Protestant like ourselves.

Who were those who finally became our family? There was old Brigid. I am not sure she wasn't the first to come. For her old bones were very creaky; she was always feeling poorly, very poorly. But in our hallway by the kitchen door we always kept a keg of porter, and this for Brigid was the finest medicine in the world. Steadfastly every day she came and sat in our kitchen, for one day we would surely see that she was just right for our film.

The next to come was Maggie, the Woman of Aran, with her madonna face framed in her black shawl. Perhaps she came so readily because she was poor and had a crippled husband and four children to provide for. Her husband having broken his back carrying a load of kelp without a donkey to help him, it was Maggie who now had to carry these heavy loads. It was the fairies who broke her husband's back, said Maggie; they threw him off a cliff, that's how it was. The fairies also steal children—not girls, but little boys. Maggie dressed her boy in skirts to outwit the fairies.

Maggie was one of the blessings of this blessed isle. She taught me about potatoes, the way—when I saw potatoes actually come as if by magic out of a layer of soil no thicker than a rug laid on the limestone—she cupped them in her hands and crooned over them, "Ah, the beautiful praties!" She had no cow for milk for the children. But when Christmas came and we gave her a cow, this only confused her—for what if the children got used to milk and then the cow might die? We had a Christmas tree, and set it up on the cement floor of our cottage. Christmas morning when she saw the tree there, Maggie crossed herself—she thought it had grown through the floor in the night.

As you can see in the film, we almost drowned Maggie. But that was not the only time a wave caught her. There was another time, much worse. Maggie's back was bent under a heavy load of kelp. She was staggering under it, making to climb up a ledge from the sea. Bob and I had already had our own experience of those ledges. We had climbed from a lower to a higher one barely in time to look down and see the ledge we had left overwhelmed to a depth of six feet by a sudden swell of the sea. It is told on the Island how thirty men were fishing along the cliff edge one calm summer day when a wave rose up and picked them off, every one. We watched Maggie anxiously; we were too far for her to hear us, for any warning cry. We saw the wave coming. I think I shut my eyes. There was an awful moment; then Bob by my side gently said, "It's all right. She's safe." And I opened my eyes and saw her flattened on the ledge under her load of kelp, like a wrack of seaweed herself, half drowned. She had managed to cling to some part of the rock and resist the backward surge of the great wave as it left her.

An important member of our family was its major-domo, Pat Mullen, our go-between between the Islanders and ourselves, and coach for our cast. After the film was over Pat took pen in hand for the first time in his life and wrote a book about it, *Man of Aran*.[2] It is the classic account of making the film; it is the feeling of the people about it; it is his feeling about it; a portrait of Bob; and there is the sweep of the Irish imagination in it and a tang of the sea.

Evenings when we sat before our big Aran fireplace with the little peat fire glowing there, listening to an Aran story-teller tell old tales of Ireland, usually in Gaelic, it was Pat who would translate them for us. These tales, as everyone knows, are of queens and kings, of giants whose heads reach the stars, and "between their legs you can see the wide world," and there is a great stirring in them of great deeds. This oral literature, this poetry, repeated over again, always marvellous, is for these people a spiritual food.

For our boy of Aran we chose Michael Dillane. Michaeleen's mother wanted him to become a priest, and this truck with Protestants was for her a very worrisome thing. I had to drink several cups of tea with Mrs. Dillane, and Michael became the proud possessor of a bicycle, the finest Bob could buy. Michael was a "broth of a boy," a daredevil and a bit of a show-off.

Tiger King, the Man of Aran, was our most difficult catch. A great tall figure with dark, curly hair like a Spaniard, he looked something like a gypsy and had a fey air about him. Aranmen ride

2. Mullen, Pat: *Man of Aran*. New York, Dutton, 1935.

Breaking rock and bringing soil for their garden.

"Tiger" King—the man of Aran.

Maggie Dirrane—the woman of Aran.

Maggie and Michaeleen. The fishing boats are coming home!

their horses bareback, sitting far back on the horse's rump like a circus rider, sideways. We would hear a great galloping along the road; it would be Tiger King lashing his horse as he approached our cottage, passing it at high speed and looking the other way. One day there was a wedding, a time of celebration, of tea and biscuits for the women in the kitchen; but for the men there was poteen, a potent potion. Tiger was practically unconscious when at last Pat brought him to us, and Bob got out his camera and we made a screen test of our hero.

Last but not least, there was Patch Ruah, Red Patch, Patch of the red beard. Patch was our animal man; he had a great way with our turkeys, pigs, donkey, and two little kids. Patch's beard was magnificent, long, red, and silky. One day we got old Patch into a curragh and put him into the film. Patch was beyond himself. "Now why," said he to Pat, "would they be wanting me in the film?"

"Well, I dunno, Patch," said Pat, "but perhaps it's because you have in you some of that drama they are always talking about."

"Drammer?" said Patch. "And where would I be having it in me?"

Pat thought a while, looking Patch over. "Well now, Patch, maybe," said he, "it could be it's in your beard you have it."

From then on there were times we would lose Patch; he would disappear, we couldn't find him. One day as we were shooting, Pat, with his fingers to his lips, motioned me to come over. He was standing beside a big boulder. I looked behind the boulder. There was old Patch sitting there, with a bit of cracked mirror in one hand and a bit of broken comb in the other, carefully, lovingly, combing his beard.

We had two main sequences to do, a land sequence and a sea, or storm, sequence. First the land sequence: how could we express the feeling of the people for their little plots of land they make with so much labor, first breaking the rock, sledging it to make a bed, then laying on it soil and sand—handfuls of soil wherever they can find it on the island between its rock crevices—then laying over that seaweed, one load after another of the heavy, wet kelp they have to bring up steep rocky slopes from the sea? In my mind I see again the raging figure of a man against the sky, standing on a hilltop, looming like a giant as he cursed and threatened the life of a neighbor who he believed had taken from his little plot a handful of its soil.

Three times we shot the land sequence, shot the whole sequence through on three different locations. Twice we failed; the camera gave us nothing. We put the sequence aside and went ahead with other scenes. Finally, when the film was almost finished, we tried the land sequence a third time. The people were the same, the action was the same; there was nothing we could think of to do but simply try another location. This time—what it was I don't know, whether it was the light that day, or the location, whether it was the way the figures moved, their relations to each other and to the land— or something else—whatever it was, it was a mystery, there was nothing we could explain about it, but at last it was there, we had it, the camera had found it. Often we would come back from a day's shooting happy and excited, sure that we had shot some wonderful stuff. Perhaps as we neared home Bob would take a pot shot at something, anything at all, just to use up the tag-end of film in his camera. Like as not the stuff we had thought would be so wonderful turned out to be nothing at all, while the pot shot, so casually taken, would turn out to be a revelation.

It was the same with the storm sequence, which Pat in his book has described so magnificently. Aran villages dot the shoreline of the Island at those points where there is a launching and a landing place for curraghs. And each village has its picked crew who pull the oars together. With each storm that came we took our cameras and our long lenses to one of these villages. Each village and each crew had its chance to show us what it could do. Perhaps one would be better for the camera than another.

"He [Bob] would see a spot in the distance," says Pat, "where he would figure he should put up his camera. Well, nothing could stop him getting there. He made a direct line, and he'd bolt through a field of briars, you know, that would hold a bull—that sort of way. He had that fire in him, you see—say nothing, but do it if it costs you your life." We worked and the men worked, returning time and time again to bend to their oars and prove their skill in the Aranman's never ending contest with the sea.

And as we shot, we developed and projected. And after the intense excitement of a day with the men and the great seas, at night in the projection room we would see it all again on the screen and our spirits would sag. As Pat put it, "Though it passed all right, it didn't look half as thrilling to me as it was when I was in the curragh doing the work. I don't know how Mr. Flaherty felt, but I was thoroughly discouraged. We even tried the other islands (there were three of them), and couldn't get anything done that was worth while—anything, that is, with this elusive dramatic quality which seems so necessary for the making of a good film, that finishing touch, the touch that goes between a good piece of work and the work of a master . . . That evening he called me into the Big Room. I went in and sat down. He was drinking his black coffee as usual. He looked at me with an unspoken question in his eyes. I said, 'Yes, it must be Bungowla and Big Patcheen Conneely!'"

Now, Bungowla is a shore on the western side of the Islands where the Atlantic swells roll in free and unbroken from the farthest reaches of that ocean. They roll up against cliffs three to four hundred feet sheer. At the base of these cliffs is a shelf of rock jutting out beneath the surface. By this shelf the waves against the cliffs are borne upward in great walls of water and spray and spume that top the cliffs and fall in a drifting curtain of mist beyond them.

It makes one of the most spectacular seascapes in the world. Here along these reaches is the village of Bungowla, primitive, isolated, one of the last strongholds of a pure Gaelic people.

In Bungowla in time of storm, curraghs are laid up, face down on the cobbles, lashed down against the fury of the wind. We had shied away from the thought of Bungowla. "I dread the thought of it," said Bob. "I don't want any lives lost."

But here in Bungowla was Big Patcheen Conneely, master curraghman of them all, and the crew who rowed with him, had always rowed with him; knew the ground, knew each other, knew the curragh under them, knew the currents, the tides and eddies, the hidden rocks, knew the sound of the wind and the feel of the sea, and knew them as one man together.

And so one day with our cameras we stood on Bungowla shore where it steps down from cliff to ledge to giant boulder. Here we had a pick of vantages from which to get with our long lenses that "elusive, dramatic quality," the "finishing touch" for this scene.

The sky was black, the wind rising and the seas mounting, as we waited for the critical moment when the men could launch the curragh. "None of them could swim," says Pat, "but I praised their blood and I praised their generation before them, and I stirred them to it . . . It was splendid to see the canoe take the breakers. A huge sea broke over Patcheen's head and the big canoe almost stood straight up on her stern as she leaped over to fight another sea. Big Patcheen shook the water from his eyes, and as he bent to the oars for a powerful stroke he threw a quick glance toward the shore. I was laughing for sheer joy and pride of how well the canoe was being handled and how I had picked the right man for the bow. He saw me laughing and, strange as it may seem, as he drove the canoe up the next great sea, and in spite of the great risk he was taking, he laughed back at me."

This was film, spirit like this! Bob loved it, and his love gave that spirit even more of a lift. Those three men in the curragh fighting through the storm became a little bit bigger than life size. They became characters out of one of their own heroic legends, a saga of themselves.

As finally the canoe crashed on shore and the men jumped free, "A great thrill of world pride shot through me," writes Pat. "For here had been a trial of the old, old stock, and the blood still ran true."

There was a great opening of the film in London. The cast were there. They got a great ovation. There they were in the theatre and there they were on the screen, and they themselves had done it. It was their film, they had made it; it was a film to tell the world what kind of people they were. As hard as ever they worked at kelp-making they had worked at making this film. They stood up in their seats, beaming with happiness. And Pat Mullen sitting beside me, I heard him say, "And God knows tonight I am glad they are happy."

IV

IN 1946, twelve years later, we come to the last one of Robert Flaherty's four "free" films, the last film he made—*Louisiana Story*.

Lousiana Story was commissioned by the Standard Oil Company of New Jersey. Robert Flaherty, who had been making biographies of primitive peoples, was now asked to make a film of a great industrial concern.

The news of this commission came as a shock to the film industry. To think that for this highly financed, streamlined project its professional skills, its technical resources, its economic powers and controls, had been passed over in favor of a free-lance film-maker—wasn't this going back to horse-and-buggy days? The Company demurred. The films that Hollywood had made had been "superficial and flamboyant"; they had "led to misconception rather than to better understanding." What they wanted was "a classic, a permanent and artistic record of the contribution which the oil industry has made to civilization"; a film that would "present the story of oil with the dignity and epic sweep it deserved and assure this story a lasting place on the highest plane in the literature of the screen. The film would also be such an absorbing human story that it would stand on its own feet as entertainment anywhere; because of its entertainment value it would be distributed theatrically through the regular motion-picture houses both in America and abroad."

This was an exacting, if princely, assignment. What they wanted of Bob was his "hallmark," his "artistry," his "ability to portray faithfully real places and real people," to give his films "an enduring and artistic quality."

We knew nothing about oil, no more than the man in the street. Before accepting the commission, Bob said he wished to make a three-month survey of oil. The company was entirely cordial to this idea; they opened all doors, and our survey began.

We were fascinated and amazed. Baton Rouge, the great refinery on the Mississippi, perhaps at the time the greatest research refinery in the world, with its strange and often beautiful because functional shapes, was pure fantasy. Towering above all other shapes were the cat-crackers, giant robots in whose vast bellies a continuous catalytic dust-storm was whirling, turning crude oil into high octane. It was this powerful gas that, by giving to English planes their edge of speed and height over the German planes, had won the Battle of Britain—so we were told. In another carefully guarded section of the refinery we saw a machine, shining in its newness, turning out rolls of synthetic rubber. Beside it stood the dark hulk of the captured German machine from which the new machine had been modelled. Already we had two stories of world affairs, of war and peace, most certainly with "epic sweep."

We went to the Texas and Oklahoma oil fields and saw the powerful working of our own economic system. As far as the eye could see, regiments of oil derricks marched over the plains and bristled in the cities. In Oklahoma City there was a derrick rising out of the yard of the governor's mansion. Here was the symbol of America's vast production, her leadership in oil, that had come out of the American way of life, out of private property, free enterprise, and all the heady ferment of capitalism. And over it all, dominant over it, stood the figure of the oil driller, the great American craftsman, in demand the world over for the skill this vast free-for-all production had given him. Here we had another story, a great American story.

But in all this storied landscape of standing shapes what did we see that was moving, that the camera could catch? We saw flame; we saw an oil well burning; and high up over the refinery, issuing from slender stacks, tongues of flame that made a phantasmagoria of light and shadow over those aluminum-painted shapes, like a surrealist dream. We saw men watching the hands of dials mysteriously moving. A button was pressed, and somewhere high up in a vaulting pipe a valve would open or close as if by magic. Out in the oil fields we might see an oil pump, pumping up and down, up and down, in a monotony of movement broken occasionally by the shadow of a bird in flight, or a passing cloud. Oil itself, that prodigious essence everlastingly seeping through prehistoric rock deep in the earth beneath us—that was beyond sight, and almost beyond imagination. Indeed, the fascination of the oil story, we decided, was exactly this mystery and unseen magic. But how to translate this into film?

We came back to the Louisiana bayou country, to its waterways, marshlands, and cypress swamps teeming with wild life—muskrats, alligators, thousands of birds. The people of the bayous, Cajuns, or Acadians, French people from Nova Scotia immortalized in Longfellow's *Evangeline*, move about in houseboats, fishing boats, and pirogues. "We were enchanted," wrote Bob, "by these gentle, gay and picturesque people who have managed to keep the individual flavor of their culture. We were delighted with their customs, their superstitions, their folk tales of werewolves and mermaids, handed down from generation to generation. But these did not get us any closer to a film about oil."

Our survey was over. We had come to the end. There was

Bayou and marshland. The boy (Joseph Boudreaux) in his pirogue.

Robert Flaherty gives the boy a boost.

The boy sees the derrick coming.

On location. *Left to right*: Frances Flaherty, Richard Leacock (at the camera), Robert Flaherty.

nothing more to see, nothing more to do. We were spent. We had just one more last day. A kindly oil pipeline inspector who was going in his motor-boat to inspect one of his lines asked us if we would like to go along just for the ride.

What a day that was! It was the spring of the year and the Mississippi was in flood. *Everything* was in motion, carried down the flooding river—branches, whole trees, masses of debris, ducks floating on logs along with turtles. Cattle stood knee-deep in water that swirled and eddied, gurgling and sparkling around them. And then, looking up, we saw an apparition—a derrick, silvery in the sun, "its slim lines rising clean and taut above the unending flatness of the marshes," and *it, too, was moving*. Suddenly this familiar sight had become a wonder. It became "movement and rhythm, the essence of all things lovable"— became, in a word, motion picture. Bob sat down and wrote to the Company the opening for his film:

> We open the film on the scene as we might see it from the bow of a canoe. We are deep in the Bayou country of Lower Louisiana. It is the high-water time of the year—the country is half drowned.
>
> We move through a forest of bearded trees. Through the gray moss dangling from the limb of one of them, a possum peers down at us. There are wild fowl everywhere, in flight and swimming in the water—herons, ducks, geese, egrets and red-winged blackbirds fly up out of our way.
>
> We are spellbound by all this wild life and the mystery of the wilderness that lies ahead. Suddenly from out of the shadow of a wide-spreading old oak a pirogue glides into a patch of water just ahead of us. In it is a little Cajun (Acadian) boy. The pirogue he paddles, the narrowest, crankiest we have ever looked upon, is hardly longer than he is himself. He paddles slowly, for he is hunting, peering to this side and that, trying to see what he can see.
>
> We cut to the details of various things as he goes on, bubbles shooting up mysteriously in the water, the vague outline of a garfish scurrying out of the way, snake birds watching him from the branch of a cypress overhead, a row of turtles on a log, tumbling in one by

one as he approaches. A little coon high up in the crutch of an old oak peers down at him. The boy smiles up at the coon. We cut back and forth from the coon to the boy, until the boy resumes his paddling and goes on through this wonderful scene. A water moccasin slithers out of his way; he pays it not the least attention.

We keep following close behind the little boy. He is as appealing a lad as we could wish to look upon—alert, graceful, ready for any adventure. He is not too old, an off-stage voice tells us, to believe in fairies, in charms, and the mermaids that swim up into the bayous from the sea. He can tell the weirdest stories of the *loups-garous*, the werewolves that on dark, moonless nights dance in the marshes. He'd never think of going out on these moonless nights without a bag of salt or a live frog, never. But there is one night when the werewolves from every nook and corner of Louisiana foregather in the marshlands for their annual ball, and all the live frogs and salt in the world would not save him then.

Robert Flaherty was a born story-teller, one of the greatest story-tellers, said John Grierson, he ever knew. I think his friends were puzzled that his films were never stories. They would gather around him at his club; when the club was closed they would adjourn in a body to the nearest restaurant, and when that closed, go on to their favorite pub until way into the morning hours, just listening to Bob's stories. The stories that Bob loved to tell, that held us all spellbound, would so often have a touch of fantasy about them. He would end them with a final "twist," like a chuckle or a smile, as much as to say, "This is just a story I've been telling you, make no mistake. It may be true—I venture to say it *is* true—but, all the same, I have made a story of it. That is all it is."

Louisiana Story is autobiography. It is Bob remembering his childhood with his father, a mining engineer, on the Canadian frontier searching in the earth not for "black gold," that is, oil, but for the true shining golden metal itself. The wonder of this world in the mind and heart of a boy is the truth of the film and its enchantment. Also it is accompanied by a miraculous story-telling score. It is not, like *Nanook* and *Moana* and also *Man of Aran*, a purely visual experience, for we have words, dialogue to which from time to time we stop to listen. But still Bob's search was for movement and how to tell his story through the camera. So soon as we started shooting, long dialogues, soliloquies, and other verbal devices bequeathed to us by our survey began dropping away (out of our minds), and more and more the lovely movement of the life around us—of birds, alligators, 'coons, of fishing boats and oil barges, and the coming of the derrick and the ballet of the drill pipes going down—took their place.

That life is movement we all know. But we can see how deeply this is so in a beautiful film[3] which shows us under the microscope the rhythmic flow, the measured movement, in protoplasm, the primordial stuff of which we are all made. When this movement stops, the measure that measures it still goes on unbroken, and when movement begins again, we see it come in, like music, on the beat. The beauty of this film is its simple and profound approach to this rhythmic mystery, taking us on the one hand into physics and chemistry, and on the other into the realm of philosophy, re-ligion, poetry. Leonardo da Vinci says, "Where there is warmth there is life, and where there is life there is the movement of love."[4] The movement of love, the mysterious rhythm of life—this is the life of film. Take, for instance, the hands of the potter as he molds the clay. The motion-picture camera can follow these movements closely, intimately, so intimately that as with our eyes we follow, we come to feel those movements as a sensation in ourselves. Mo-mentarily we touch and know the very heart and mind of the potter; we partake, as it were, of his life, we are one with him.

3. *Seifriz on Protoplasm*, by William Seifriz and J. M. B. Churchill, Jr. Copyright 1955 J. M. B. Churchill, Jr. Distributed by the Educational Film Library Association, 250 West 57th Street, New York 19, N.Y.

4. From the commentary of the motion picture *Leonardo da Vinci: Man of Mystery*. (Pictura Films Distribution Corporation, 41 Union Square West, New York 3, N.Y.)

Here, through those nuances of movement we found in *Moana*, we come again to that "participation mystique" we found in *Nanook*. Here is the "way" of the camera, of this machine: through its sensitivity to movement it can take us into a new dimension of seeing, through the mysterious rhythmic impulses of life and love take us inward into the spirit, into the unity of the spirit.

Robert Flaherty let the camera see everything, avid as a child, filled with a childlike wonder. His pet word was "marvellous." Everything was marvellous, and his enthusiasm was equalled only by his patience. Patient as a scientist, he let the camera see everything exhaustively, and then, you remember, he brought all this to the screen, and screened and screened it, and went out and shot again, for one reason only: to give the camera a chance to find that "moment of truth," that flash of perception, that penetration into the heart of the matter, which he knew the camera, left to itself, *could* find. The point in this process was that it was purely visual. Words played no part in it; it went beyond words. It was simply a degree of seeing. As ice turns to water and water to steam, and a degree of temperature becomes a transformation, so a degree of seeing may become a transformation.

I experienced such a degree of seeing in Samoa. Samoa was my first experience of living, as Bob had lived so long, with people of another culture. They were a friendly people. When we met they greeted me, "*Talofa!*"—my love to you. We would talk a little, perhaps about their children and my children. They would say, "*Manuia*"— God be with you—and I had absolutely no feeling of being alien to them. Until this thing happened, and happened so suddenly, like a clap of thunder or a flash of lightning, that I remember it exactly, and exactly how I felt, as suddenly everything seemed to fall away from me, everything but the immediacy of that moment, and the presence, the overwhelming presence, of these most lovely people. For the first time I saw them. I saw them as I had never seen them before. And not only that: I saw every least thing as though I had never seen it before. It was as though I had come to some sort of threshold, and stepping over had come into a new world and found myself a new person.

This experience I have come to think of as my initiation into the motion picture medium. For Iris Barry, who founded the Film Library of the Museum of Modern Art, says of the motion picture: "Its particular property is a sense of discovery, like that of an astigmatic person who sees a new and richer world when he first puts on his spectacles—a sensation of delight in seeing something with new depth and penetration, as if for the first time."

And Pudovkin says much the same thing: "The basic aim of cinema is to teach people to see all things new, to abandon the commonplace world in which they live blindly, and to discover at last the meaning and the beauty of the universe." Both Iris Barry and Pudovkin use the word "discover." To them the motion picture medium is discovery, and by that token it is poetry. "Poetry," says Sir Herbert Read, "being exploratory . . .'

To the Eskimo artist his art, too, is exploratory. One who knows him well describes the Eskimo artist at work:

> As the carver holds the unworked ivory lightly in his hand, turning it this way and that, he whispers "Who are you? Who hides there?" And then: "Ah, seal!" He rarely sets out, at least consciously, to carve, say, a seal, but picks up the ivory, examines it to find its hidden form and, if that's not immediately apparent, carves aimlessly until he sees it, humming or chanting as he works. Then he brings it out: Seal, hidden, emerges. It was always there: he didn't create it; he released it; he helped it step forth.[5]

I had the opportunity recently of seeing four films of Robert Bresson, and my eyes were opened to the great similarity, and the

5. Carpenter, Edmund, *et al: Eskimo.* Toronto, University of Toronto, 1959, p. [33].

41

great difference, between Robert Bresson and Robert Flaherty, two film-makers each in his way pure. Both of them are seeking the spirit, the inner life, the interior. Robert Bresson begins with the interior, and then he makes or creates an exterior to fit it. Robert Flaherty, on the other hand, begins with the exterior and *discovers* the spirit that is in it, like the Eskimo. In the Eskimo language "there are no real equivalents of our words to *create* or *make*, which presuppose imposition of the self on matter."[6]

So there are these two ways, the way of making and creating, with its discipline of *doing*, and on the other hand the way of discovering, or releasing, with its discipline of *letting be*.

The great main stream of film-making goes the making, the creating, the fiction way, for that is our habit of mind. But Robert Flaherty's whole life was a passionate and stubborn fight for the exploratory way—for a natural poetry, for a greater awareness of the essential truth of things as they are, a deeper communion with all being. His only care was that his films should show these values which the new medium had brought into the world. With every film he hoped that the *next* one might be great enough so that people would see—see that the approach to the medium which could bring them these values was the natural approach, true to the nature of the medium, true to its function and its destiny.

Robert Flaherty never made a love story, the ordinary love story, boy-meets-girl. But out of his camera, whatever the subject, love came of itself, spontaneously, love *extra*ordinary, so that John Houseman could say of his films, "They are rooted in love."

Love is a celebration. Robert Flaherty celebrates the free spirit of peoples. He celebrates his own fight for freedom to make his films. But above all he celebrates a new and strange and perhaps portentous fact, in the history of art a "first": that the liberation of the spirit that comes from the profound experience of any great

6. Carpenter, *loc. cit.*

art can now come to us in a mass medium for a machine age through the mediation of a machine. "On the spiritual plane, cinema is an invention every whit as important as on the material plane, the freeing of nuclear energy."[7]

Love's method is surrender, the giving up of the self to that which is greater than the self, in order that the greater, the beyond, may come through. Surrender is the discipline also of the scientist, *his* humility, *his* search into the nature of things. Robert Flaherty has been called a mystic. Lillian Gish likened him to the poet Blake. John Grierson said his attitude to the camera was that of a mystic. Robert Flaherty was a mystic of the modern age; in his approach to a powerful machine he took the scientist's discipline of "surrender to the material and surrender to the tool" in order to come to the mystic's ecstasy and delight, and to his wisdom.

7. Debrix, Jean: Cinema and Poetry. In *The Art of the Cinema.* (Yale French Studies, no. 17) New Haven, Payne & Lane, Summer 1956, p. 101.

ROBERT FLAHERTY:
CHRONOLOGY

1884   Born on February 16 at Iron Mountain, Michigan, son of Robert Henry and Susan (Kloeckner) Flaherty.

1899–1900   Attended Upper Canada College, Toronto.

1902–1903   Attended Michigan College of Mines, Houghton.

1910   Led first of four expeditions into the Hudson Bay area under the sponsorship of Sir William Mackenzie. Explored and mapped Belcher Islands.

1911   Second expedition.

1913   Third expedition. Films made during this expedition were later burned accidentally in Toronto.

1914   Married Frances Hubbard, daughter of Dr. Lucius Lee Hubbard.

1915   Fourth expedition.

1921   Began again to film Eskimos.

1922   *Nanook of the North* released.

1923   Commissioned to make a picture of real life in the South Seas by Jesse L. Lasky of the Famous-Players-Lasky Corporation (Paramount Pictures).

1924   First book published, *My Eskimo Friends*.

1925   Experimental short film, *The Story of a Potter*, released. Worked on experimental short film, *The Twenty-four-dollar Island*; never completed for release.

1926   *Moana* released. John Grierson first used "documentary" to describe Flaherty's approach to film-making.

1928   Went to Tahiti to collaborate in the direction of *White Shadows* for Metro-Goldwyn-Mayer, but withdrew from the collaboration.

1929   Began work as author and co-producer with F. W. Murnau on *Tabu*. Withdrew before the film was finally edited and released.

1931   *Tabu* released. From Berlin, failed in attempt to obtain permission to make a film in the U.S.S.R. Invited to London by John Grierson, who produced a film *Industrial Britain*, directed by Flaherty, and released the same year.

1932   Went to the Aran Islands to make a film commissioned by Michael Balcon, of the Gaumont-British Corporation.

1934   *Man of Aran* released. Awarded first prize at the 1934 Venice Exposition.

1935   Went to India on commission of Alexander Korda to make film of Kipling's *Toomai of the Elephants*. Co-director, Zoltan Korda.

1937   *Elephant Boy* released.

1938   His book *The Captain's Chair*, a novel, published.

1939   His book *White Master* published. Invited by Pare Lorentz to make film in U.S. on soil erosion and agricultural displacement.

1941   *The Land* completed, but distribution restricted.

1942   Filmed sequences for the War Department.

1946   Commissioned by the Standard Oil Company of New Jersey to make film associated with their activities.

1948   *Louisiana Story* released. Recognized at the Edinburgh Film Festival and received a British Film Academy award.

1950   Given honorary degree of Doctor of Fine Arts by the University of Michigan.

1951   Died July 23 at his home in Dummerston, Vermont.

1953   Robert Flaherty Foundation established with headquarters in New York City.

1954   Foundation headquarters moved to Brattleboro, Vermont.

BETA PHI MU CHAPBOOKS

This book, THE ODYSSEY OF A FILM-MAKER, has been published in an edition of two thousand copies. The text has been composed in English Monotype Bembo and printed on Curtis Rag paper by Clarke & Way at The Thistle Press in New York. The plates are by Publicity Engravers of Baltimore. The binding is by the Russell-Rutter Company of New York. Format by Bert Clarke.